# LEE TREVINO
## THE GOLF EXPLOSION

Junior High Library
Brandywine Public Schools
Niles, Michigan

# LEE TREVINO
## THE GOLF EXPLOSION

## by Julian May

Published by Crestwood House, Inc., Mankato, Minnesota 56001. Published simultaneously in Canada by J. M. Dent and Sons, Ltd. Library of Congress Catalog Card Number: 74-82743. International Standard Book Number: 0-913940-08-9. Text copyright © 1974 by Julian May Dikty. Illustrations copyright © 1974 by Crestwood House, Inc. All rights reserved. No part of this book may be reproduced in any form without written permission from the publisher, except for brief passages included in a review. Printed in the United States of America.

Designed by William Dichtl

**Crestwood House, Inc., Mankato, Minn. 56001**

## PHOTOGRAPHIC CREDITS

Horizon Corporation: 13; United Press International: 2, 8, 10, 11, 16, 19, 20, 23, 24, 25, 28, 30, 33, 34, 36, 37, 38, 39, 41, 47, 48; Wide World Photos: 6, 14, 17, 18, 22, 26, 27, 29, 32, 35, 40, 43, 44, 45, 46.
Cover: United Press International.

# LEE TREVINO
## THE GOLF EXPLOSION

A little boy prowled in the weeds. He crept along the edge of the golf course, searching.

Suddenly there was a gleam of white. Grinning, he picked up a golf ball. It was a good one, not cut. He tucked it into his pocket with others he had found.

Three men—well-dressed, well-fed—were playing the seventh hole. The boy waved and one of the men came over to the fence.

"Hi, Mex!" he said. "Got any good ones today?"

The boy reached into his pocket. "Six good ones. Six bits."

The man handed over the money. "Don't spend it all on comic books," he said jovially. "See ya, Mex."

The little Mexican-American boy would not spend the money on comic books. He would spend it on food for his family. They never had enough food.

No one, looking at the boy, would guess that some day he would be a millionaire. Or that golf balls and clubs would carry his name: Lee Trevino.

The old house where Lee Trevino lived as a boy in the 1940's once stood on this spot, now the 14th hole of the Glen Lakes Country Club in Dallas. The house was torn down some time ago. Lee was born December 1, 1939.

Lee lived with his mother, his two sisters, and his grandfather, Old Joe. Their home was a run-down shack near the Glen Lakes Country Club of Dallas, Texas.

Old Joe worked as a gravedigger. Lee's mother was a cleaning woman when she could get the work. The Trevinos were very poor.

One day, Lee found a golf club. An angry golfer had thrown it over the fence after missing a shot. Old Joe cut down the club to fit little Lee. He showed the boy how to swing.

"There! Now you will be able to play the same game as the rich gringos," Joe said.

Lee went prancing away with the sawed-off club. He swung at pebbles, at weeds, even at horse apples. So this was golf! He decided it was fun.

The next time he went ball-hunting, he brought one home. He cut down the tall grass and made a hole out of a tin can sunk in the earth.

"Look!" he said proudly to Old Joe. "Now I have a golf course all my own!"

There were no other boys living nearby for Lee to play with. So he practiced golf.

And sometimes, when the moon was bright, he climbed over the golf course fence. He played on the beautiful green lawn of the country club—and dreamed that he was rich.

Hardy Greenwood, owner of the driving range where Lee worked, was the first person to encourage young Trevino to make a career of golf.

Lee quit school in the eighth grade and went to work. He caddied at the country club and helped mow the grass. When he could, he played a little.

Then he got a job at a golf driving range. The owner of the range liked Lee. The boy was cheerful and he worked hard. But as Lee grew older, he became restless.

His boss said, "Lee, you could earn a good living at golf. You're getting to play like a real pro."

But Lee only laughed. Then he joined the Marines.

Lee Trevino was 17. The year was 1956 and the United States was at peace. The poor boy from Texas discovered that he loved boot camp, loved the traveling, loved everything about the Marine Corps.

His great sense of humor made him a lot of friends. Even the officers liked him—especially after they found out about his golfing. Lee became a rifle instructor and rose to the rank of sergeant. He played in armed-services golf tournaments in Japan and other Far Eastern countries.

When he was ready to leave the Marines, in 1960, he had made up his mind to become a golf pro.

Lee often hustled at the Tenison Park Municipal Golf Course in Dallas. He would show up in shabby clothes, barefoot, and bet that he could play a better game than some prosperous-looking victim. If Lee had lost those bets, he would not have been able to pay up. But he didn't lose!

Lee went back to work for his old boss at the driving range. The salary was small—but Lee had other ways of making money.

He would bet people that he could drive a golf ball accurately using a Dr. Pepper bottle for a club. And he would do it!

Or he would dress shabbily and go to the public golf course. There he would lure somebody into playing for money—then win the bet by playing a fantastic game of golf.

He got married, but he refused to settle down. Instead of staying home with his wife and baby, he fooled around with his friends and spent endless time golfing. The marriage ended in divorce.

Lee played in some small tournaments. But in order to go for the big prizes, he would have to be accepted into the Professional Golfers' Association. And to get a PGA card, he needed the help of his boss.

The owner of the driving range refused. He said, "Lee, you're just not *steady* enough."

Lee was deeply hurt—and mad, too. He was a great golfer; his private life was his own business! He quit his job at the driving range. After a while, he got married again. His second wife, Claudia Fenley, helped him to grow up. He stopped hustling and began to think about his future.

In 1965, the Trevinos moved to El Paso. Lee became assistant pro at Horizon Hills Country Club.

The beautiful clubhouse of the Horizon Hills Country Club in El Paso, where Lee worked as an assistant pro in 1965. He earned $30 a week. Strong desert winds make the course a difficult one.

Horizon Hills was a rough course. A fierce wind from the desert blew over the fairways much of the time. It was at Horizon Hills that Lee developed a special swing. It was a low, line drive that stayed under the wind.

As a pro, Lee had to teach other people how to play. But he himself had never had a lesson. Because of this, he had a rather strange style. He would point his feet to the left and swing to the right. It was a funny-looking stroke, but it usually sent the ball where Lee wanted it to go.

13

In 1966, the owners of Horizon Hills helped Lee get the long-desired PGA card. At last he was eligible to play in the big tournaments!

He went to play in the U.S. Open in San Francisco. Without decent clothes, playing with unmatched clubs, Lee showed 'em what a poor Texas boy could do.

He came in 54th.

He slunk back to El Paso, where Claudia tried to cheer him up. But he felt terrible. There were only two legal ways he could make a living at golf: One was as a resident pro, teaching people to play. He was doing that now—and earning $30 a week. The other career was that of a touring pro, traveling from tournament to tournament. In this, the sky was the limit.

But only if he was good enough.

He renewed his practice. Still, when the 1967 U.S. Open came around, he refused to enter. Claudia sent in the $20 entry fee herself. She forced him to go to Odessa, Texas, for the regional qualifying round. He came in first with a 69.

The next round was in Dallas. He shot a great 67. His scores made him the best local qualifier in the country.

His confidence had returned by the time he went to the U.S. Open itself, in Springfield, N.J.

There, as a complete unknown, he played against the nation's top pro golfers. To everyone's surprise, he came in fifth and won $6,000.

The U.S. Open is played in June. Instead of going back to El Paso, Lee decided to play in other tournaments around the country. Short and stocky, cracking jokes and making faces, he became a favorite of the fans in the gallery.

Autograph seekers crumble the fence surrounding the 18th hole at the close of the 1967 U.S. Open. Lost in the mob are Arnold Palmer and Jack Nicklaus, crowd favorites. No one was interested in the autograph of the man who came in fifth—Lee Trevino.

He played in 14 more tourneys in 1967 and won prize money in 12 of them. The year before, his earnings had barely lifted him out of the "poverty" bracket. But in 1967, he made $27,000 just by hitting a little white ball better than a few hundred other guys!

Claudia shared his pride when Lee Trevino was named golf's Rookie of the Year.

"Lee's Fleas" watch him practice.

His playing, especially his putting, improved greatly during the first part of 1968. Nerves still bothered him sometimes, however. He was tied for first place on the last hole of the Houston tournament. All he needed to do was sink a four-foot putt.

Later, Lee admitted: "I couldn't even see the cup!" He blew the putt and finished second.

By the time the U.S. Open rolled around again, Lee had already earned some $50,000 in prize money. He had also acquired a devoted band of followers who cheered him as he played. They would become known as "Lee's Fleas."

The 1968 U.S. Open was held in Rochester, N.Y. On the first three rounds, Lee shot 69-68-69. It was good enough for second place. The leader, by a single stroke, was Bert Yancey.

In the final round, Lee and Bert were paired as partners. Two more different men would have been hard to find. Bert was tall and fair, an icy-cool player who had gone to West Point.

And then there was Lee! People now called him the "Merry Mexican." He was always yakking and laughing it up with the gallery. And when it was time to hit the ball, he used strokes that made the old-time pros wince with horror.

Bert Yancey with Lee Trevino at the 1968 U.S. Open.

Lee and Bert began the final round. On the third hole, Lee shot a par three while Bert Yancey missed a putt for a bogey four. Now Lee and Bert were tied for the lead.

Lee's Fleas shouted *"Ole!"* whenever their hero did well. By the time the first nine holes had been played, Lee had pulled ahead by one stroke.

On the eleventh hole, Lee sank a beautiful 35-foot putt. Bert Yancey dropped behind by two strokes. On the next hole, Lee finished with a 20-foot putt that gave him a four-stroke lead.

*"Ole!"* yelled the Fleas.

But Lee wasn't finished yet. Before the day was over, he led Bert Yancey by six strokes, finishing with a one-under-par 69 for the 18 holes. It was the first time a golfer had played all four rounds of the U.S. Open under par.

Bert Yancey finished third with a total of 281. Second was Jack Nicklaus, with 279. And the winner, with a 275 that tied the Open record, was Lee Trevino.

When they handed him the first-prize check for $30,000, he said:

"I'm gonna use it to buy the Alamo and give it back to Mexico!"

Lee does a typical little dance after sinking a 20-foot putt in the 1968 U.S. Open. After a good shot, he has been known to leap, screech, throw his hat away, and even fall down flat. His lively ways endeared him to fans who were bored by the cool tactics of other pro golfers.

He went on to win more money, including a first prize of $25,000 at the Hawaiian Open. His former tour room-mate, Hawaiian pro Ted Makalena, had been killed in a diving accident. So Lee donated $10,000 of the prize money to a trust fund for Makalena's son. It was not the last time he would give large sums of money to causes he considered worthy.

He was a warm-hearted man—and now, at last, he could afford to be generous. He earned a remarkable $132,127 in 1968. And it was only his second year on tour.

Lee's wife Claudia gives him a victory kiss after the 1968 Hawaiian Open.

Now sports companies wanted to name golf equipment after him. He was invited to invest in real estate. He had to hire a manager to look after his business interests. He even made commercials for Dr. Pepper, remembering the money he had won hitting trick shots with soft-drink bottles.

Early in 1969, he won the Tucson Open. People who had sneered at him as a clown and a fluke winner began to fall silent. Lee Trevino liked his fun, but he was also a splendid golfer with a style all his own.

A bird for a missed birdie. Lee shows his disgust after a ruined putt.

For the first time, he was asked to play in the Masters Tournament. It was a great honor—golfing's equivalent of being summoned to a royal command performance.

But Lee Trevino had his doubts. The Masters was loaded with prestige. Only the best golfers were invited to play in the tournament. But it also had elements of snobbery that Lee mistrusted. And it was held at the segregated Augusta National Golf Course—a beautiful place that was also very hilly and difficult.

Lee played with misgivings and finished 19th. "I'll never play that course again," he said. "It's just not my kind of place."

Lee and two caddies study the green during practice at the Masters Tournament in Augusta, Georgia.

The large gallery at the 1969 Masters parts to allow the immortal Arnold Palmer (white shirt) to approach the first green. He won the Masters four times.

Lee said some things about the Masters that made a lot of golfers angry. Later he apologized—some said because the PGA forced him to.

But the next year, even though he was invited, Lee Trevino did not play in the Masters. And in other years when he did play, he did not win.

What was the trouble? Perhaps the beautiful, rich man's course stirred up some bad memories in him. Perhaps it was the sight of all the black caddies and black waiters—but no black golfers—that reminded him of prejudice he himself had faced as a Mexican-American playing a gringo's game.

Lee poses with his family. From left to right: his mother-in-law, Mrs. Lou Loare, his daughter Leslie, Claudia Trevino holding Tony, and his son Richard.

The life of a touring pro is a restless one. If he wishes, a tournament golfer can spend almost the entire year "on the road," going from course to course. The constant traveling is a strain on the golfer—and on his family, too.

Driven by a desire to prove himself, Lee entered as many tournaments as possible. Sometimes he was able to bring Claudia and their two young children along. But all too often, the family had to stay home in Texas while Lee played in some distant city.

That fall, Lee teamed with Orville Moody, winner of the U.S. Open, to take the World Cup match in Singapore. Lee's score was the best in the tournament, which matched the top golfers from some 50 different countries.

In 1970, Lee won the Tucson Open and the National Airlines Open in Miami. But he faltered badly in the U.S. Open, tying for seventh. The surprise victor was an Englishman, Tony Jacklin.

Hankering for revenge, the Yankee golf pros—including Lee Trevino—challenged Jacklin at the 1970 British Open. It was played in Scotland, where golf was invented, on the St. Andrews course, oldest in the world.

At the end of the third round, Lee was the leader by three strokes. In a three-way tie for second were Jacklin and Doug Sanders and Jack Nicklaus of the United States.

Lee drives off at the British Open in 1970. At left, in the plaid slacks, is British golfing star Tony Jacklin.

Jack Nicklaus hugs his wife, Barbara, after defeating Doug Sanders in a playoff to win the 1970 British Open.

The dignified British didn't quite know what to make of Lee. Some of his jokes—such as spitting on his golf glove and then shaking hands with the Prime Minister—seemed to them in poor taste.

But the final joke at the British Open was on Lee himself. He forgot that the tricky fifth hole at St. Andrews has two cups on a double green. He made his approach to the wrong one. By the time he corrected his mistake, he was socked with a bogey that lost him the tournament. Jack Nicklaus won the title in a playoff.

By the end of his third year on tour, Lee had earned $157,037, more than any other golf pro. But that didn't mean that he was happy. Despite the fact that he never dropped his funster image, Lee was a worried man, and his golf showed it.

Some of his outside business ventures were failing, eating up his money as fast as he made it. His marriage was becoming more and more strained by the long absences. And on top of everything, his beloved mother was dying.

To save his marriage, he agreed to take a three-month vacation from the tour. To help relieve his other cares, he took to visiting hospitals for crippled children. Cheering up kids helped cheer Lee up, too.

By April 1971 he was a changed man. He went back on tour full of the old spirit and won the Tallahassee Open. This was followed by another tournament win and a collection of high-place finishes, and he was in a fine humor when the U.S. Open came around again.

It was played at the venerable Merion Country Club in Ardmore, Pennsylvania. Lee brought along a set of mink-trimmed tees and gave everybody fair warning:

"There are 16 birdie holes here and 18 bogey holes. I'll eat all the cactus in El Paso if anyone breaks 280."

During the first part of the tournament, a young amateur named Jim Simons led the field. As the final round began, Simons had a score of 207, Jack Nicklaus had 209, and Lee 211.

The three of them stayed close together until Lee birdied on the 14th hole and took the lead. He stayed ahead until the last hole, a par-three.

There he drove into the rough. A beautiful chip shot put him within 7 feet of the pin. If he sank the putt, he would win the Open.

As he addressed the ball, the gallery held its breath. Then—*smash*! A young boy perched on a ladder fell off and spoiled Lee's concentration. The ball missed the cup and Lee finished with a 280 score.

So did Jack Nicklaus. The two great golfers faced a playoff round on the following day.

Lee blasts out of a sand trap during the 1971 U.S. Open. The Band-Aid on his forearm covers the name of a former girl-friend.

Both players were very tense and Lee had to do something about it. As he came up to the first tee, he reached into his bag and hauled out a realistic toy rattlesnake. As the crowd squealed, he threw it at Jack.

"I need all the help I can get!" Lee cried.

Nicklaus thought the snake was very funny. The tension was broken and the playoff began.

A bogey and a double bogey by Nicklaus gave Lee a two-stroke lead. A brief storm stopped the game at the sixth hole. Then Jack momentarily drew closer, and the rivals were only a stroke apart at the ninth.

Officials at the U.S. Open were not very amused by Lee Trevino's snake, but everyone else thought it was hilarious. Here Lee pretends to kill it with a hatchet he pulled out of his bag.

Jack Nicklaus congratulates Lee on winning the 1971 U.S. Open.

A bogey by Jack on the tenth allowed Lee to regain his two-stroke lead. What followed was an exciting birdie contest in which the old champion played splendid, under-par golf—only to have the Merry Mexican do even better. Each time Jack threatened, Lee responded with a birdie of his own.

The deciding hole was the 17th, where Nicklaus fell into a sand trap and lost still another stroke. The last two holes were played at par, with final scores of 71 for Nicklaus and 68 for Trevino.

Afterwards, Lee said: "I'm a lucky dog. You gotta be to beat Jack Nicklaus, because he's the greatest golfer who ever held a club."

Lee chips out of the rough during a tense moment in the 1971 Canadian Open.

Two weeks later, at the Canadian Open, Lee seemed to falter. He trailed veteran pro Art Wall, Jr., by two strokes as the final round began.

But on the very first hole of the last round, Lee eagled on a par-four hole! He was even with Wall and he stayed that way. At the end of the 18 holes, the rivals were tied, 275-275.

The Canadian Open has a sudden-death playoff. It took Lee only a single hole to wrap it up.

With two championships under his belt, he raced for the airport to try for a third in the British Open. He cried: "Tell them Supermex is on the way!"

Only three golfers—Ben Hogan, Gene Sarazen, and Bobby Jones—had ever won both the U.S. and British Open in one year. No one had ever won a triple crown of U.S., Canadian, and British titles as Lee Trevino proposed to do. His main rivals were Nicklaus, Tony Jacklin, and an amazing golfer from Taiwan named Lu Liang-Huan. He was called "Mister Lu" by everyone, and Lee had played him before—when he was with the Marines in the Far East. Then, Mister Lu had whipped young Lee.

By the end of the third round, Jack Nicklaus had dropped out of contention. Lee led with a 208 while Jacklin and Mister Lu were tied for second with 209.

Lu Liang-Huan of Taiwan jigs with delight after going in front momentarily in the third round of the 1971 British Open. But moments later, Lee Trevino took a one-stroke lead in the tournament.

Lee and Mister Lu were paired in the final round. Supermex birdied the first hole. While Jacklin double-bogeyed the second, Lee made par. Keeping up a line of comical chatter, he hatched three more birdies on his way to the sixth hole.

He hung onto his lead all the way to the 17th hole, leading Mister Lu by three strokes and Jacklin by four. It seemed like he had the title sewed up. . . .

And then he hit a sand hill. He tried a wedge shot and got nowhere. Then he blasted out of the sand— only to land in the rough. A bad chip and a worse putt left him with a double-bogey 7.

Going into the last hole, his lead over Mister Lu was reduced to a single stroke.

Lee explodes out of the rough, displacing a big, shaggy divot in the process. Spectators watch in misty weather at Southport, England, site of the 1971 British Open.

Lee made a good drive, while Mister Lu nearly landed in a bunker. The Chinese golfer's second shot bounced off a woman spectator's head right onto the fairway. He finished with a birdie and a score of 279.

But good as Mister Lu was, Supermex was better. He putted to within two feet of the pin, then pushed the ball in for a 278.

Gleefully, he threw his cap into the air and raced across the green to hug Claudia. He had won his triple crown.

Former title-holder Tony Jacklin, who came in third in 1971, rates a hug from Lee at the conclusion of the 1971 British Open.

Usually sunny Las Vegas had temperatures in the low 40's, forcing Lee to play in cold-weather gear. Here he signals a successful 35-foot putt, which helped him win the 1971 Sahara Invitational.

Tired out, Lee played poorly at the Western Open and at the Westchester Golf Classic. He decided to take another vacation—only to suffer an attack of appendicitis.

It was not until October that he was back in playing form. He went to Las Vegas, where bitter cold and strong winds made a nightmare out of the Sahara Invitational. Playing in a floppy rainsuit, Lee said: "I don't care if I shoot 85. I'm not going to get pneumonia!"

He toughed it out and won. The prize money brought his 1971 total earnings to a whopping $227,243.

Jack Nicklaus and Lee smile after winning the 1971 World Cup match for the United States.

Another triumph came his way in November. He and Jack Nicklaus teamed up to win the World Cup for the United States. And to wind up his greatest season, he was honored with no less than four "Athlete of the Year" citations.

Along with this glory went a rare kind of fan devotion. An admiring fellow-pro pin-pointed Lee's appeal when he said: "The golf tour is like a big circus that pulls into town once a year. And Lee is the ringmaster and clown rolled into one."

Lee himself knew another reason why the fans liked him. "I represent the average guy," he said, "the garbage truck driver, the mechanic, the guy who goes to the driving range. I swing just like they do!"

In 1972 Lee surprised everybody by announcing that he would play in the Masters. But he wouldn't go into the segregated clubhouse and locker room. He changed his shoes in the parking lot.

And he played all wrong, finishing 33rd. The winner was Jack Nicklaus, who also went on to beat Lee in the U.S. Open. Nicklaus was hoping for a grand slam that year. To do it, he would also have to win the British Open and the PGA title.

Both Lee and the gallery register delight as the Merry Mexican wraps up the 1972 British Open.

Lee was at the British Open, of course, to defend his title. And so was Tony Jacklin.

At the end of the third round, Lee was leader by a single stroke over Jacklin, as a result of having made five straight birdies!

Jack Nicklaus was six strokes back. But he played brilliantly in the final round, first passing Jacklin and then closing in on Lee.

Nicklaus managed six birdies on the first eleven holes. But then his luck deserted him. Lee kept a firm grip on a one-stroke lead and won the tournament with an ancient pitching wedge, chipping in from the rough at the edge of the green for a final birdie.

Jack Nicklaus exclaimed: "Trevino, you're something else. Why don't you go back to Mexico?"

And he was only half joking.

Many a great athlete suffers a slump. And this fate now befell Lee Trevino. Jack Nicklaus had warned that Lee would "burn himself out" with his hectic tour schedule. And his words seemed to come true. The British Open victory was to be Lee's last major title for a long time.

He still remained a money-winner, however. "Maybe it's time to retire," he said. "But first, I'm going to make my million."

He went to the 1973 Masters hoping to lick his jinx and become a millionaire in a single crack. He did well until the last round—then blew it all by shooting an abominable 80.

So his goal of making a million was postponed for a month, until the Danny Thomas Classic in May. There he went over the top. Sadly, it was as runner-up, not the winner. Dave Hill won the tournament.

After that, Lee complained of being tired. He devoted much more time to his businesses and to his family. He went on tour again in 1974, but had won only once by the time the PGA tournament came up in August. This contest, like the Masters, had always slipped away from Lee.

At the Danny Thomas Classic, played in Memphis in May 1973, Lee registers pain as his putt fails to drop. His second-place tie finish was good for a prize of $16,187.50, giving him a career total of $1,001,889.47.

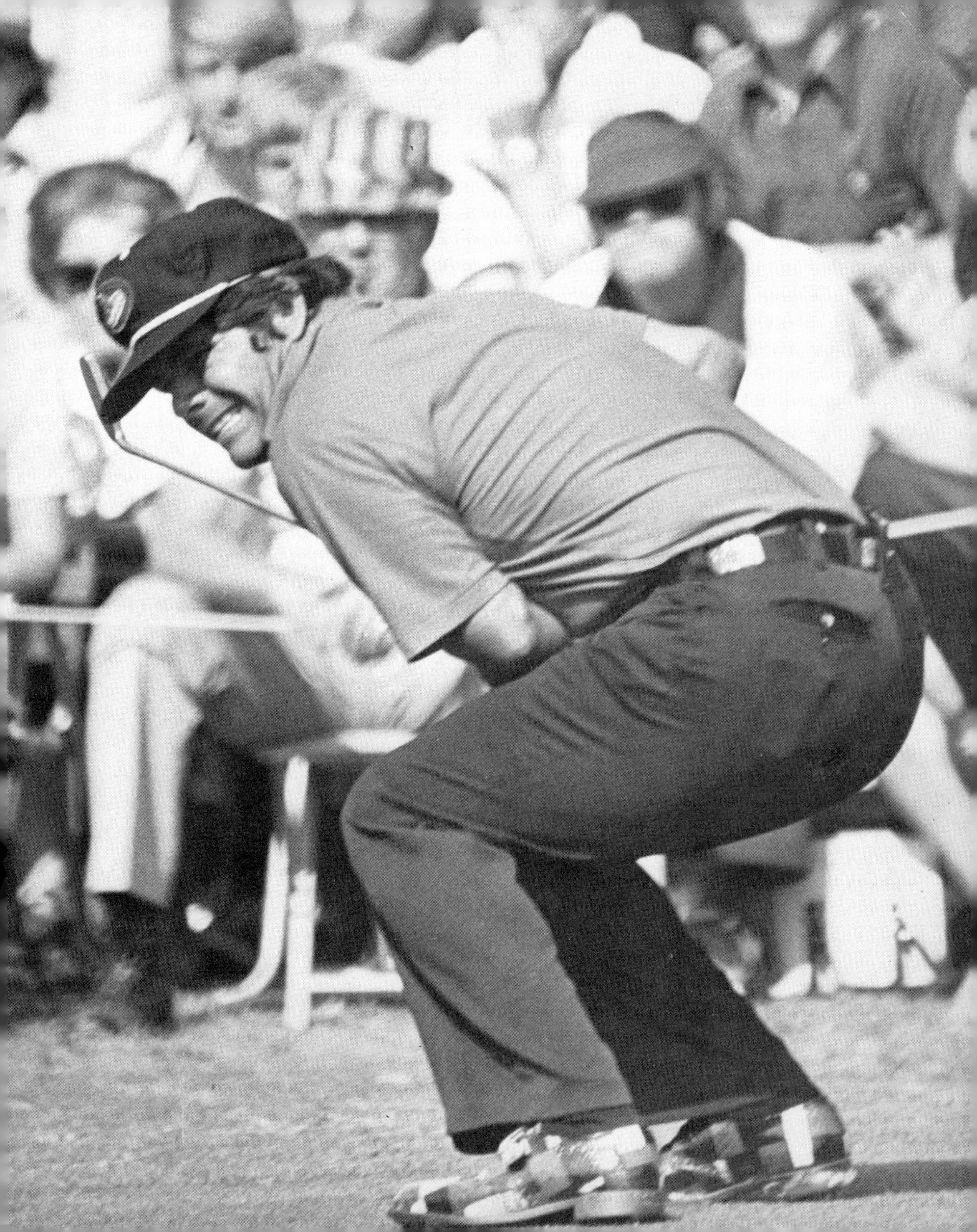

Lee comes out of the sand.

The 1974 PGA tournament was played at Tanglewood in North Carolina. Rain turned the fairways soggy and Lee, getting the feel of the unusual course, shot only 73. People wondered if he was still tired.

On the second round, Lee socked a juicy 67 in spite of the drizzle. "Ain't nothin' like a low round to make you un-tired!" he said happily. Nevertheless, that day belonged to South Africa's Gary Player, who came up with a record-tying 64.

On Saturday, in the third round, the men began to be separated from the boys. Lee got a 68, his birdie on the 18th hole putting him ahead of another South African, Bobby Cole. Cole tied for second with Jack Nicklaus, a single stroke behind Lee.

Lee wasn't laughing when the third round ended. He said: "I'm going for broke tomorrow. I've never been this close to the PGA before. I may shoot 65 or I may shoot 80—but I'm going for broke!"

The last day of the tournament was hot and humid. Young Bobby Cole managed an eagle on the first hole. Then Lee birdied. Nicklaus bogeyed the third, then came in one-under-par on the fourth and fifth holes. Then he absent-mindedly put his putter into Lee's bag.

"You trying to stick me with a two-shot penalty?" Lee asked, dumping out the extra club. "Tell you what: I'll take the two if you promise not to use that putter for the rest of the round!"

Jack Nicklaus cringes after missing a birdie at the 1974 PGA Tournament.

Cole fell behind and it was Trevino versus Nicklaus all over again. Both great players approached the last green, Lee leading by a stroke. If Jack could manage a birdie, he would tie the tournament. But his putt missed the hole.

This is a happy face—honest! Lee takes a two-stroke lead in the 1974 PGA.

A joyful Lee Trevino holds his first PGA trophy.

All Lee needed to wrap it up was par four. Two strokes had brought him to the green. Then he putted—a foot short.

Turning to Nicklaus and his playing partner, Hubert Green, Lee pleaded: "Fellas, if you don't mind, I'd like to play out of turn. I want to scrape this ball in. I just can't stand to wait here lookin' at it."

With the others agreeable, Lee Trevino sank the putt and won his first PGA crown by a single stroke. His final round score was 69, for a total of 276.

After it was all over, Lee offered to buy a round of cool drinks for all the players.

"I will, that is," he said with a grin, "if anybody can cash a check!" And he waved his $45,000 first prize.

Everybody, including Jack Nicklaus, laughed.

There was no doubt about it. Supermex was up to his old tricks once more.

On September 9, 1974, Lee Trevino won the World Series of Golf tournament at Firestone Country Club, Akron, Ohio. He won on a sudden-death playoff against Gary Player.

**DATE DUE**

| | | | |
|---|---|---|---|
| MY 26 '76 | JA 26 '99 | | |
| MY 28 '76 | FE 12 '99 | | |
| DE 1 '76 | OC 14 '99 | | |
| FE 7 '78 | MY 12 '00 | | |
| DE 12 '78 | | | |
| OC 21 '81 | | | |
| OC 31 '85 | | | |
| FE 01 '93 | | | |
| JAN 29 1996 | | | |
| MY 12 '97 | | | |
| JA 29 '98 | | | |
| FE 20 '98 | | | |

B  May, Julian          copy 1
Trev  LEE TREVINO: THE GOLF EXPLOSION

Junior Library
Brandywine Public Schools
Niles, Michigan